In the Common Dream of George Oppen

Joseph
Bradshaw

In the Common Dream of George Oppen

First published in the United Kingdom in 2011 by
Shearsman Books
58 Velwell Road
Exeter EX4 4LD

www.shearsman.com

ISBN 978-1-84861-149-8

Cover: *Homage to Albers* (digital media) by the author.

Acknowledgements
Some of the poems and essays from this book were first published (mostly in earlier versions) in *Cannibal, Cultural Society, Denver Quarterly, MiPOesias, Mirage #4 / Period(ical), Shifter, Tarpaulin Sky,* and in the chapbook *This Ocean, or Oppen Series* (Cannibal Books, 2008).

Contents

Addenda

If, on that beach, on that jagged shore where one sees, if you encounter a tree . . . one must acknowledge that tree – – – what's there

—George Oppen

In
the
Common
Dream
of
George Oppen

A kingdom is a simple thing
A place where doors usurp their keys.
One can laugh there at the gate
And then enter or walk away

A kingdom is these breaking things:
A stony beach, the unmoving edge
One sails a life to see, to sit
In the open, waiting for a tree

A simple thing, an easy tree. Crossed out
A simple cross — Can it then be borne
Across the gaping kingdom
We give all our life to see

Crossed out. Having given
All our life to the sea, we wait
For a pillow to fall upon us
In knots of sleep.

Incipit

In the beginning there was a man named George Oppen. His biography was well known: a poet who abandoned poetry for war, who spent 25 blank years before filling another page, who then wrote himself into a coterie of young admirers, won a Pulitzer, became senile with Alzheimer's, and died scratching vague aphorisms into the wall of his nursing home (*The world is black magic / The world is half magic*). Yet not much was known behind these facts of a life. The only thing certain about him was that he had written many poems, and that some of them, such as 'Of Being Numerous,' were very well respected. All of his poetry was, after his death, put in a book called *New Collected Poems*. In a review of *This Ocean, or Oppen Series*, an earlier version of *In the Common Dream of George Oppen*, Chris Piuma wrote:

> There is, of course, no poem called 'Hell' in Oppen's *New Collected Poems.*

And, later:

> To be sure, there is no poem called 'Our Own Private Idaho' in the *New Collected Poems*, nor even a mention of Idaho.

This then raises the question: In those 25 blank years, did George Oppen visit the green shores of Idaho? If he did, what impact would this have had on the poetry he wrote after those 25 years? Who, looking back across the abyss of those unwritten times, will fill their blankness? And will we arrive—will we find—our first, bright century waiting just ahead of us if we descend into that immemorial—

I'm getting ahead of myself. Let me begin again.

In the beginning there were no questions, and thus no need for answers. It was not until stories started being told that mysteries arose. And as the stories were passed from generation to generation, what was lost in forgetting, censor, and mistelling, was precisely the foundation for common understanding. There came, instead, a lurking in variation, alternate endings, beginnings, middles—all of them interchangeable. It was as if every dropped twig sprouted a new tree.

There was then a forest of stories told—all of them more or less the same, but none of them corresponding. Many poets became lost in that dark wood. Some called it Hell, and some called it Paradise. William Blake called it a Tyger. So, after Blake, Oppen addressed this place of vagary in a poem called, appropriately enough, 'The Poem:'

> *to save the commonplace save myself Tyger*
> *Tyger still burning in me burning*

In the forest George Oppen was burning from the inside out. It was as if he had fallen in the darkness, his foot caught on an exposed root, and the "commonplace"—that is the common place, the forest—had at his touch caught flame. Tangled in those roots, Oppen's legs burned. And then his arms burned, and then his torso, and then his toes and his hair. Then his face burned, and then his hands. And as his hands burned, and as the tree he was caught in and all of the forest's birds burned, their flames in turn ignited his name, and—lastly, slow—it burnt from his body. So we probably can't even speak of George Oppen anymore.

But in the beginning there was a man. He told us that, in the beginning, we have to choose the meaning of beginning—i.e., we must choose our own myths. Here are our choices:

a) In the beginning there was a child who, holding a mollusk's shell up to her ear, first uttered the word "ocean," which started the flood that still soaks us to this day.

b) In the beginning there was "Narcissus, who because he could not grasp the tormenting, mild image he saw in the fountain, plunged into it and was drowned."

c) In the beginning there was Oppen who wrote, "I've never read [Jack] Spicer, but will."

d) In the beginning there were echoes, and the thud that started them: A lone minotaur—startled at a glimpse of his own image—dashed out of the cave and, stumbling at the cliff's edge, fell into the canyon. The thud was Plato's laughter.

e) In the beginning there was a startle. I woke in the Waremart in Caldwell, alone, finding myself sorting through the notebooks in the stationery aisle, which I begin to notice were all filled with the markings of a familiar hand.

And now, having chosen—if we can choose—we begin at the beginning, offering a line to Oppen from the opening Canto of Dante's *Inferno*:

> *Tu se' lo mio maestro e 'l mio autore*

Translation:

> You are my teacher and my author.
> These hands that father yours
> have pricked, have vivisected me—

As we proceed, include this dedication in the spaces to come: between wrenched trans- and shaky ab-duction—between the dismembering of the forgotten, still lurking, and the constitution of false memory—this is the beginning:

But that wasn't the beginning. In an earlier version of '*Incipit*,' the phrase "this is the beginning *colon*" is followed by "we must find our lyrical necessities." These words were scratched out. In an even earlier version, "this is the beginning *colon*" is followed by a summoning of Dante at the outset of *Vita Nuova*, when he writes, "I will copy into this little book the words I find under that heading,"—i.e., of *incipit vita nova*—"if not all of them, then at least their significance." It then went on to reference Ovid's tale of the flood, in which "stray birds, searching in vain for a landing, tumble exhausted into the sea." They are moments of beginning anew and ending defeated: a house is built and another destroyed. But the line drawn between them, if it was even a line, has been scratched out; therefore this, the beginning, is where we begin:

Host

Necessity lyrical to find
neighbor's window broke.

As chimney formed from smoke I go
to cicadas, alfalfa
the distance of house from where
feet'd tremble is Idaho, a coming
Host to wing smashed into
you takes no stepping light

finding it harder to sleep at night.
Cold bed's to be bartered
&'s retarding, as the woe
of two round a tree—

one falls the other
fells, ahoy timber to follow
what hands or house one brings.

---

cf. Robin Blaser's 'Cups': *two poets in a tree is clearly / the same thing as poetry.*

Boise

Bark, in Idaho, was
the stripping of fingers seen through
a mirror, green

from alfalfa traces. The landscape
buckling, readjusted
were your fingers what cannot

grip, folded
in Idaho these leaves
were carried through, across from

you. In Idaho
that city of trees I see
hands touching water, a river

to wash my fingers of
absence, what should be you or
I, in Idaho.

'Hell,' by George Oppen

'Hell,' by George Oppen, may not exist. Look at the palimpsestic draftsheet of 'The Extremes,' reproduced on p. 351 of *New Collected Poems* (New Directions: 2002). What we see resembles a geological maelstrom: torn and scissored typewritten sheets are pasted and taped together, then handwritten over (and were, incidentally, to be torn and pasted even further: 'The Extremes' is an early draft of 'Anniversary Poem'). What we're calling 'Hell,' however, is materially incoherent. Is it the projected wall between pastoral memory and Oppen's 'Idaho'? Or is it an *ad hoc* structure which we frieze into the significance of our house?

'Idaho,' by George Oppen

In Idaho, that soiled green,
Was the green of tree, the was
Of Paradise and everything.

When you entered your feet
Were a sign among the roaming
Waves pounding ashore in Idaho. In that sea

Birds culled a word called
Idaho from their wings. Such confusion expanding
As froth, you confused

Gulls scattering with the sea's
Flung spray. In Idaho you were
Anything, but everything, but Idaho.

-2] ~~*In Xanadu did Kubla Khan*~~
-1] ~~*A Stately Pleasure Dome decree*~~

On 'Kubla Khan'

While composing 'Idaho'—which was literally scrawled over his copy of Coleridge's 'Kubla Kahn'—George Oppen heard a scraping at the entrance of the barracks. By his own account, he went to the door and found a visitor "whose features even in that present [moment] had the blurred, nondescript quality of the memory of a face—perhaps the face of an ancient acquaintance one knew only in passing." This visitor then thrust an object into his hands, and "in the few seconds it took to discern that what I held was a worn, familiar looking notebook, he disappeared."

After returning to his room Oppen stood over his still-opened Coleridge, the ink still wet, and flipped through this "familiar looking notebook," growing all the while dizzy. Suddenly nauseous, Oppen vomited, then stumbled to his cot and passed out. Upon waking he found the following text, written in his own hand, in the notebook he had just acquired:

> *Traveling through a town called C. A strong sense of returning ~~I recognize nothing~~. I follow a man who was leaving a supermarket through a wooded area outside of the market square. I lose him halfway up a long hill.*
>
> *Trudging up it, the path gradually is murkier, stickier, slowing my step—soon I'm wading through what I understand to be shark marrow, which boils me, starching my pants. I am bewildered by my pants, amazed by the heat they keep—I am burning at the crotch.*
>
> *A long struggle with my brick pants.*
>
> *Naked finally, and unashamed, I ascend further, until coming to a kind of shed, its floor caked shin-deep with bone, crushed to powder. In the center of the dank room is a glass encasement of a large but broken animal*

skeleton, in the shape of a shipwrecked hull, labeled 'Shark Exoskeleton.'

The man is there. We both trawl through the room, looking into the case, and the powder is cool on my shins. I then notice a small radio on top of the case. As I reach for it I see the man regard me through the glass, his eyes the color of pomegranates. Tuning the radio, his lips move. They seem to say: The first time I wrote this you weren't there, but this time you are.

'You,' by George Oppen

And to go far beyond you,
sow "lyre" in "charred helicopter."
In our age of Orphic sleep, you

Call long distance on a crushed kazoo,
Reel in the teasing carrot
Once strung by this living hand

My hands, shivering
And in you I am
Breathing in the moments come
Toward—lapse—flitting

Away—
no bird without you
is a bird you

2] find the lyre hid in rabbits teeth.
12] bird] wolf
13] bird] wolf
14] *the line that's found, I cannot trace*

'That Land,' by George Oppen

Sing like a [...] *at the open. If*

Once thought to be part of Oppen's series 'Five Poems about Poetry,' 'That Land' traced the impulse to reckon time back to a pre-calendrical state, when some 13,000 years ago a certain Cro-Magnon woman stood in the forest of the mythic North, in what is now the Dordogne Valley in central France. It is said that Oppen, writing from a far shore, portrayed her clad in deer hide, carving careful notches into an eagle's femur bone, in what was apparently the first effort to record the moon's cycles. Like this bone calendar, the poem—the one line that remains of it—is left to us broken, fossilized ...

'The Cruelties,' by George Oppen

Deformed I don't woman
Memory, I keep hope in my will

she brings a paradise green as O
the was that greens the tree—
the sea of was is everything.

Should I wait inside her, hurt
she bleeds many through as I
bleat her through my thing,
and I waste in, taste in her an away—

Can any bird light its own wing?

It's these cruelties, I know, that seam the hem
of being: the sky low, as cattle moan
in pastures opaque in feathered flutter,
the clouds are you to earth's I

where feet are rooted firm, the birds
are thick, amiss as she
unmends the interinanimate sheet till
uncovered, she's gone, and I am

A

stray hair to the
wind through the open
O, autumn

leaves scuffing the flickering E in Applebee's
fall, fill a space no longer claused
in roots, what was I

in waiting
for the remarkable   *Tune of the ragged birds beaks*
                            In the tune of the winds (Oppen)

marking the missing near
as love's breath smudged in mirror, an ear
to unpresuppose tongue—

'Bird,' by George Oppen

Were the [...] heard approaching
Never arriving [...] we trail after
Never catching the [sound] we thought we heard
Fathers voice trailing off [...]
In present moments
Of nearly being present with you [...] not running after
But sitting still and waiting for you to [pass] through
A four of hands unfolding palms
Reflect refract
A face almost familiar among
So many familiar faces lips open close
Open soundlessly Father
Father unseal your throat

In a moment of lucidity unusual in his last years, 'Bird' was written on the wall of the room where Oppen died. The poem had been partially erased (assumedly by Oppen), and over it was scrawled (downward, diagonally) the two lines: *The world is black magic / The world is half magic.*

On *The Book of the Third*

for Jordan Stempleman

Relate this dream: A stranger (who was my closest friend) crawled through my window, into my bed, pressing against my chest a copy of Oppen's *The Book of the Third.* I awoke, puzzling through it, recognizing here and there snippets of lines, fragments of memories: Have I read this before, or are these memories already mine? There was much indeed that was familiar, yet the book was wholly alien to me. I wanted to stuff it deep in a closet, under years of soiled socks and pants I know I'll never wear again, but there was no such space available—I am alone with this book. The scene around me—my room, all objects in which I recognize myself—faded, and I was left only with these pages, with my hands' grasp of them. As if independent of my will, they opened to a poem called 'The Kingdom:'

There is ease
of accustomation, and then the ease of
drying the neck and arms,

drafts of presence, then forgetting
the tiny hill to our house of 7,
the creek that was a canal—

Will my image resettle
after I've fallen in, my shoes still on—
Does it still run on—

There's no place to begin, only, or singly
false endings, billowing
through the curtain, beyond the window—

Here, I can keep our thoughts to myself,
hide them in the klinks
of bottles and voices from the street—

Here long after our goodbyes, or
having settled in to the smell of one another's feet,
what we came to see we find was

crossed out, it was
not a thing, and not even
a thing's thousand strings, but

shadows of mounds of
slithering, suggesting string, suggesting
an unseaming of being—

Crossed out,
do we tug the frayed ends of this tangle till
undone, and you are no longer

what drives us through this landscape of having been,
of thighs in a tire-swing, rubbed raw,
in a dry raft—

I have stopped my reading, struck by the thought that, as I read, I had somehow skipped over the many first person pronouns in the poem. I look back through the passage again, noting:

I was uncomfortable in it until
my body heat saturated it—

And I'm struck by something else: Did I actually see these last two lines in 'The Kingdom,' or are am I reading them for the first time? I read on:

Toward Idaho, beyond memory

my fingers press the forehead,
slowly lifting an eyelid, yet
not enough to reveal the eye—

I am dizzy, tugging at the hairs of my brow,
and write the elephantine swell of
a cello's drone, I am dizzy

dizzy as the green of currency,
as the swirling layered
waves crashing down upon waves

crashing down upon waves,
innumerable threads complying to,
or jamming the loom—

'The King,' by Joseph Merrick

My hand folded inside my overgrown hand is the King of remembering's wrinkle. In there snug, he's jailed, yet home; but if I clench, he's crushed like a paper cup, he's a nest of clipped wings, an awkward thing.

Thus the King is sentenced to days spent in dark imprisonment, released only in burst moments, only in waves—I wave neither goodbye nor hello, but simply acknowledge whatever passes.

An eye, like a hungry safe, swallows and keeps the things it sees. At times, while passing the King, he meets my gaze, and my eyes glaze over, locked into what was seen. His mouth then opens, ready. Touching my hand with his lips when I blindly extend—as if prostrate—the King grips, squeezes.

Joseph Merrick is the author of *Rippling Evasions.* Due to the congenital disorder known as Proteus Syndrome, which caused abnormal skin overgrowth and tumors over most of his body (the only parts unaffected by the disorder were his genitals and left hand), he was referred to as "The Elephant Man," the name by which he is more commonly known.

In Conversation with George Oppen

I first became interested in George Oppen when, by chance, I came across the opening of his poem 'West:' *Elephant, say, scraping his left hand / Against his cage, as his other hand passes, says yes // This is true.* These lines struck me on a deeply personal level. I felt that Oppen had perfectly, quietly, articulated the horror of my somatic situation—my constant horror. I then contacted him, and a warm correspondence ensued, and eventually Oppen agreed to sit down with me in his living room for an interview. But after it was conducted I felt a deep ambivalence about transcribing and publishing it, so the tape sat on a shelf for many years, centuries even, and over the course of time the vicissitudes of technology had their way with the tape. When I decided to finally transcribe the interview, I discovered that much of it had been overtaken by another recording: the voice of George Oppen either reading or perhaps dictating a poem or notes of some sort. Whether the tape was simply being recycled and, in its deterioration, an older content was resurrected, or whether Oppen's voice had been transferred onto the tape from some ultimate, unknown place—I'm not sure. I can only indicate that I've attempted to distinguish these two Oppens by dividing his voices into (*italics*) and (roman), before posing—as a sort of epigraph—the question: *Who will be the third that speaks always from below us?*

—Joseph Merrick

[beginning of tape *]*

George Oppen: *One is entirely alone, in the company of men. Amidst the laughter, the friends, one is alone. Even in the reach—*
Is it on?

Joseph Merrick: Yes. I'd like to begin by speaking of returning. Much ado has been made of the fact that you gave up poetry for other concerns, and then returned to it 25 years later. What brought that to bear?

Oppen: I've talked at length about this in other interviews, so for now I'll just say that it was a dream I had about my dead father that brought me back. The dream's recorded in 'Blood from the Stone.' But the 25 years weren't silent. During that period there were of course the years of war, and Mary and I lived and worked and traveled many places; but above all there was the single poem I worked over, again and again, which, even through all the assembly and disassembly, I just couldn't pin down.

Merrick: You're referring to 'Our Own Private Idaho,' right?

Oppen: Right—that long arc of stray arrows . . .

Merrick: And where is the poem now?

Oppen: Well, there is no such poem, and in a way there never was. There were instead many drafts, endlessly unfinished. And they're all gone now—I buried them. It was the only way to be finished with it.

Merrick: Where did you bury them?

Oppen: In an undisclosed location, as they say. Only Mary knows the place.

Merrick: You won't tell me where it is?

Oppen: No.

Merrick: Could you then talk a little bit about it? Twenty-something years is a long time to spend on a poem no one will ever read . . .

Oppen: I'm not sure that much can be said about it. It started out about my mother, who died of suicide when I was quite young. *When a woman lives here, she is a hand, king of the puppets, a hand folded in the house folded, or crushed like a paper cup, a nest of wing . . .*

Merrick: . . . does Idaho play into the memory of your mother?

Oppen: It's purely associational. Even the word "mother" brings up various images which have nothing to do with the actual person. I found, as I started the first drafts, that every time I wrote the word, images of Idaho's landscapes would pop into my head, as if floating behind *this good house. An ocean is a woman who lives untouched* to bring this association into the poem, conflating these two disparate things—these two displaced things. That's possibly where it all went awry. *Yes, all constitutes the thing, all that is discarded in its making. Pages crumbled into a book, crumpled as the house and the woman in the house, folding things . . .*

Merrick: . . . that when you started trying to work with these associations, the poem went awry. This was still early on in its composition—but why did you keep at it?

Oppen: New things would come up, which would seem relevant to the constellation I was trying to identify for myself. One thing I remember—not a particular memory, really, but a general sense I had about myself at the time my mother died—was that everyone around me was really a wolf, and they were all sent from some unseen place to observe me. I remember thinking that when they were out of the range of my sight they would assume their natural, lupine form. But when I could see them—whether I was interacting with them directly or not—they were in human skin. I thought it was their disguise—to make themselves look like me. I would often sit with my mother, and play a kind of peek-a-boo with her—turning away, hiding my face, and then springing back toward her as fast as I could. I wanted to see if I could catch her without her disguise.

Merrick: Did you?

Oppen: I thought I did. I'm sure she thought I was just being a normal kid. She probably had no idea what I was doing. [*laughter*]

Merrick: I'm curious to know how all these memories factored into the poem.

Oppen: So am I! Honestly, I can't tell you. The wolves were just another wrong turning . . .

[Jack Spicer]: Another five years . . .

Merrick: Who said that?

Oppen: Who said what?

Merrick: That voice just now—

Oppen: What voice?

Merrick: I heard something...

Oppen: I don't know what you're talking about.

Merrick: He said "Another five years."

[Spicer]: I can't see the birds, the island, anything but vacant twists and shifts of the tunnel . . .

Merrick: Did you hear him this time?!

Oppen: No, I didn't. [*laughter*]

Merrick: He was talking about a tunnel.

Oppen: A funnel?

Merrick: A tunnel.

Oppen: *Here, where the first river ran or spills ashore, there is a glass. Filled with amber, this glass mirrors a clear, empty glass. One glass sits on the sill of a windowless house, the other is called Xanadu. Everything here comes crossed out* as if everything of Idaho was a projection, a construct.

Merrick: Right, that fits the history of its name. In the 1860s a Rocky Mountain Senator, George Willing, suggested this newly acquired landmass be called "Idaho," which he claimed was a Shoshone word meaning either "the sun comes from the mountains" or "gem of the mountains." The name stuck, but some years later Willing admitted that there was no such Shoshone word—he had made it up himself.

Oppen: Ha! What a hoax! I guess "Idaho" may as well mean "the hoax of memory" now, right!

[laughter, then silence *]*

Merrick: OK, this seems a good time to return to silence. In 'Of Being Numerous' you have the well known line, "Clarity in the sense of silence"—

Oppen: Yes, there is that, but there are many other silences in my work—or I should rather say *attempts toward* much that we must pass over *the wolf formed from clay hands stuffing mouths with* silence—this is our only chance of actually coming to understand *the waves of wing that brush against, that crash into a face. The wound, salted, a transparent white, transparent white* . . .

Merrick: I'm not sure I follow you . . .

Oppen: "Clarity in the sense of silence" is a silence of horrors—of seen horrors. We see them, or hear them—all of this on the radio, the television—but we cannot speak to them. They are beyond us, these images—

[Spicer]: I once wrote an entire poem without a single bird in it.

Merrick: There's that voice again!

Oppen: [*sighs*]

Merrick: Do you have the windows open or something?

Oppen: Um, I don't think we do . . . Should I continue?

Merrick: Yes, I'm sorry . . .

Oppen: As I was saying, we can no longer accept these images. We need to look for the world around us—the actual—the real birds, trees, our company. For—

[Spicer]: Yep, not a single bird in it.

Merrick: You had to have heard him this time.

Oppen: Actually, I *I* was trying to say something . . .

Merrick: He said "not a single bird in it." You didn't hear that?

Oppen: Not a single bird in what?

Merrick: I don't know! I can't believe you didn't hear it! It's so clear!

Oppen: Joseph, there's no one here except yourself and myself. Mary's out right now, but she's making tacos later if *I remember my mother in the garden by the sun-dial and the Rothfeld grandmother who asked me not to play the piano so loud and I said* a narrative interrupted by the wolves of faded poems—

[Spicer]: Metaphors are not for humans.

Oppen: But I've often admired your beautiful *flashing eyes, his floating hair. Take his right hand and weave a circle round him thrice . . .*

Merrick: Wait—you can hear him?! I thought you said—

Oppen: Hear who?

Merrick: That voice! What did you just say was beautiful?

Oppen: I don't know what you're talking about.

Merrick: But didn't you just say his good hand was beautiful?

Oppen: Actually I was referring to yours. I've often admired your beautiful *In that flame can one see a child's hair? I can no longer see . . .*

[end of tape *]*

An Apocalypse of George Oppen

This is true: Metaphors were the earliest animals. At death (and only at death) they would learn to move their mouths, emitting for the first and last time an oceanic roar—a caw of naked waves here, expired flesh there. While some listeners claimed to hear their names in the sound of a dying metaphor, it has been thought that the sound cried out in an animal's final moment was the sound of *its own* name.

But do you know why George Oppen called his boat Bird? Rachel Blau DuPlessis, who rode upon that boat, who watched Oppen at the helm, has written:

> George is on the sea, steering, the sea pulling: the poem changes force and weight at every word but moves continuing forward.

This is clear: Oppen's Bird is the vessel of poetry. But DuPlessis has her remembrance of Bird, her remembrance of her Oppen: a man of flesh, gasps, hiccups, speech and belches—an American man with whom she spent American afternoons on porches and beaches, in bodies removing themselves to discretely shit elsewhere, away from the talk, the humor, the exchanges of warmth and overstepping of bounds. It is not my Oppen.

My Oppen is that mythical lacuna, that self-doubt so evident in these words never meant to be read by another:

> 25 dead years. I am trying to return 25 years: the breaking that becomes the way birds become. ~~Cross it out~~ ^*eradicate the first gesture*^ I cannot remember a single line. I can only remember the magnificent violence of the birds, their notorious violence—

^It is all wrong. ~~*I can only see the notorious violence of*~~^

^*Scratch it out. I can only see what I cannot*^

Oppen hesitated—at the mouth of the ravenous, ragged birds, whose hands would not be struck blind (mute)? But by cutting Oppen's hands and placing them into mine (I meant to write "under mine," but didn't) will I be able to see and speak? If I assay *past* this infinite series of misspellings, these gestures toward a primitive anamnesis, even while I imprint upon the page what haunts the peripheries of memory—

The last sentence is all wrong. Leave it unfinished—

This is true: *This Ocean, or Oppen Series*, though unfinished, had been published. I sent copies to several poets, including Rob Halpern, who replied with a poem of his own from a series called 'Some Speculations around George Oppen's Parousia.' Beginning with a line from Oppen's 'Five Poems about Poetry'—*the casual horror / Of the iron*—the poem continues as a kind of gloss:

> (By which he must have meant being
>
> Penetrated by the impenetrable thing
> Fucked & nailed to wood a beam
> Still singing of birds or stone or glass—

Here we have Oppen as a harbinger of Parousia (literally "being present"), projecting his voice skyward while hung upon a plank, his torso about to fall, yet he still (without song) sings:

> Anything to name so that by naming
> Make the thing appear to overcome
> Its own idea the gleam the unimaginable

Made of labor and hardened in the act
Of time a speech so pure so perfectly
Coinciding with the nail it avoids—

I don't want to say the word Christ. I want to say the spoken space "so perfectly / coinciding with the nail it avoids" is true, is the Orphic lighting of matter—that there *is* a matter to be found, to be unveiled in the common dream of George Oppen. So maybe Halpern's Parousia is the unveiling (literally "the apocalypse") of our dream: Oppen, us, alone together, until he is squeezed out like blood from a wound and we are left only with the traces of his hands, the smears of his hands against ours, his voice rising, off, away, melding with the cries of the birds: Oppen, our bird, scratched out, or *into* being—

On 'Myth of the Blaze'

It is said that once (and only once) in his small coastal shack, Oppen saw Blake's Tyger. He wrote:

> his eyes of flame, his hair a blink
> the Tyger is the unnamable named

Oppen was nearing death. He knew it. He knew he had been waiting for or writing toward this moment, this blink, since boyhood. As Adam named and named the animals, *the vigorous dusty strong // animals*, he never named that frightful pocket of birds that ceaselessly cut the airy way: he knew to do so meant death. And so Oppen knew that when he would finally see the Tyger he would die shortly afterward: no poet can sustain such a bright intensity, a wholly illumed sky's worth of clarity: no poet could sustain such heat.

In his small shack this glimpse of the Tyger severed Oppen's eye from his hand. The taxonomy that once held together the names of these body parts ceased currency. There was no connection between seeing and the said, between a hand and the loves it touches, between a body and a body. There were instead only bodies, plural in a singular, traumatic scape.

As the parts that were the names of names of George Oppen coagulated or floated away from each other, he looked down at the kitchen table, now fuzzy through the shower or flood of ether evacuating from the punctured birds, and he made a violent gesture. He wrote, *in the knife-cut*, stopped. His hands were bleeding. He wrote, *in the opaque // white*, and was nothing. He wrote *bread each side of the knife*, and was no longer. All that was left of him was a house. All that was left of him was *the secret taste / of being lost* in the fire.

On 'Myth of the Blaze'

They fle from me that sometyme did me seke
With naked fote stalking in my chambre.

So begins one of Sir Thomas Wyatt's poems—one of Oppen's favorites. After his battalion was killed in the War, Oppen—the last man alive—lay wounded in the Alsatian clay of his foxhole, his body flayed with shrapnel. It is said that here—as he listened to the enemy flee, abandoning him as a cold casualty—Oppen composed his legendary poem of discipleship, 'Myth of the Blaze.' Dragging his knuckles across that spattered ditch, he silently scraped the words of the poem into the foxhole's wall. While the specific content of the poem may ultimately remain unknown, we do have Oppen's account of the occasion in a letter to the Charles Reznikoff scholar, Milton Hindus: "I waited, I think, and during those hours Wyatt's little poem and Rezi's poem of hidden stars ['The Stars are Hidden,' from *Rhythms*] ran thru my fingers over and over, and the Tyger—they filled the space around me like a wolf as my nails filled with that dirt and blood . . . and I wept and wept."

As with the classic Hindu tale of the fallen master and the disciple—in which the disciple provokes the dead master awake, into immortality, through a danced constellation of symbols—we can see in this moment of crisis, disaster, Oppen, ever the disciple, dancing in the foxhole, addressing his masters through their own language, in the hopes that by awakening their words he too might wake into immortality. I have thus attempted a resurrection of 'Myth of the Blaze,' in which Oppen's address—or "mudra," if you prefer—begins with the Father, then moves to the Tyger, and then on to Mary (who, it is believed, through Oppen's own hands addressed him in return).

Myth of the Blaze

I must get out of here
Father
He thinks Father

I am not so far from I
Have sene them gentill tame and meke
That now are wyld I am

Not so far from I fle from
Me that sometyme did me seke
With naked fote stalking in my

Tyger Tyger, brenning bright
The stars
Are hidden, the lights

Are out I beat my fists against I cry
And remember
Boyhood   Mary

Therewithall sweetly did me kysse
And softly saide
Dere hert, how like you this:

I
Fle from me
I was no dreme

A Ballad to be Finished by George Oppen

Preface

As we know, the lost fragments of the Ancient Greek poet George Oppen can't tell us anything about our century. We cannot move forward into the past, even when it appears that that is what we are doing:

just feet away from trucks carrying another, his suicide vest, accounting for the highest yet, had claimed responsibility with the floodlights, explosions, caught on camera

Like tanks we advance: your Knight for my Queen, your knife for my thumb. The metaphor's bad and, as we know (I'm merely copying this), not for humans: I love you. How could Oppen possibly continue on with this?

'From the Iron Itself'

a fifteen days of Christmas kill
a *thy tonge stille / And have al thy wille*
b continues rising upward

c dramatic gestures which we knew
c the faded circles, X's he drew
b a blend of biblical birds

d on a row of rickshaws, see
d carries the painted text: Can these
b earlier, higher numbers

e their shirts were pulled, exposing ab
e your graves, and bring you into the land
b has clearly tried to under

b reported unknown numbers surv
b ter you, and ye shall live. The words
c after the storm continue

d there was a noise, and behold a shaking
d in turn evoked the memory
c cause breath to enter you

e
e
c leyde erthe in erthen through

a Can these bones live? Behold, I will
a your local NPR affil
c lapsed, yet several casu

c	
c	
d	were dragged out of a mini
e	tied wooden coffins, minivans
e	a diaper showed above the waistband
d	to enter you and ye
a	of any civilians in the vil
a	
d	shall live. The words, evoking
b	
b	
d	four winds, O breath, and breathe
d	Ezekiel 37:3
d	exploding, they said the body
e	
a	
a	
e	
b	
b	
e	
c	
c	
e	
e	
e	
a	

b
b
a

c
c
a

d
d
a

a
a
b

On 'Paradise'

The question, after the fire, will be not *what* but *where* are the birds, and how will we pronounce their names (are we permitted to pronounce our names)? *The question is: How does one hold an apple / Who loves apples?* (Oppen) Another shift in wind, a flattening out of the pasture's grasses—The question is: How could we move forward into "we," even as it appears that "we" is what we'll never be? The question—Is "is" a song (an interrogation of silence) or is it this, toward which we perpetually continue: "I love you"? When will I have written this?

Of the Fire

Our skin, which brings and steels us against unknowing
Tougher than anything.
Emptied hours of grasses in the wind
The sky, rusted above open valleys
Of fingers holding only their failure
To grasp.
Held
As if in expo-
Sition: an apple, as if
Still a tree: and you, watching us
Watch the thing fall, rippling in the pool that once
Drew us toward our image.

From a journal dated 7-6-08: "Dreamt I was rewriting 'Of the Fire,' itself a kind of rewriting of Spicer's poem beginning with the phrase 'This ocean, humiliating in its disguises.' Details murky—I may have been confused or apprehensive about why I was rewriting it. But in the rewriting there was a peeling away of the first (my) poem. I remember going over that first line word by word and each word literally falling away (from the page? the mind?)—"

The Poem

See who handled that axe?
Now say leaf, knuckle, nail

in sawdust clumped red—Say no one
sees the saw, or these responsible hands—
If the hands are seen at all

No place says the past of these hands,
what brought them to
Chop the tree then chop

the wrists—What will the house be
if not composed of this tree, what resemblance
will our hands be to keep—

House

What I couldn't write I scratched out.
—George Oppen

No body bases this proximity: a house is out of, descent to

flayed planks, charred eaves. We don't stay where we say piano,
say music's hands are burnt 4th degree. We don't say this:

Prairie salt, and smothering salt, and ocean's fauna dragged
dry as beached seaweed, bleached Idaho. Scratch that

2

A woman walks into the house. Tangled in her hair is a bird
and the pine trees where the mind starts, bending its teeth.
The woman motions for us to follow—

The dune grass matted by blackened oars, the woman points to
a woman on a burning barge, then jumps from deck. Scratch
that

3

She says her body bases this proximity: the house is a sleeping
woman, a woman with arms empty, arms stronger than flame,
that bird. We don't say that scape of the hair

Synapse. Unlet, I sit down to write I sit down and write I am standing—Am I walking

Question. Hunger, does it walk by itself, does hunger listen to itself speak of hunger—Yes, I have a sound I can't hear

How one lives indicates how well one listens. Example: I am walking to, standing by

the fridge, the corner grocery. Example: Have I heard footsteps before, behind, or with my step. Question: *wolf walks in my footsteps fear fear*

*

A ghost is felt behind the image: The ravenous, do they walk or sit, do they clutch themselves or images of furry bodies or selves—Yes, I have a stomach I can feel I have

Africa. Scratch that

An image: March 2002, two men on a train in Portland are discussing the three boys found locked in a bedroom in South Carolina, having subsisted for 8 years off of raw Bisquick and water, and, when no Bisquick was given, drywall. The lower portion of the bedroom's walls entirely eaten through

I've walked through the city—rendered in letters never fully formed, envelopes never sealed—lost among what almost sounds: the mouth. Example: the hands, do they search for clues of the mouth along the walls of a house, do they say I have entered a city, do the hands start

I have entered two cities but left only one of them. One of the cities was a house, the other the invaginate crease of a beak. This beak, it was said, led not to the mouth of a bird, but to the mouth of a hunger. When this mouth was entered, my feet ceased to mean more than one thing. Start here

A music: Does one hold a sound as one pinches a cicada between thumb and fore, the vibrating abdomen rattling the walls of the house—Yes, the house has no hands

An image: A pair of hands, this pair, found floating, mute in the suspension of freefall

(as the coyote's surprised expression, his resignation to the inevitable plunge (roadrunner offscreen))—A pair of hands dangling like a penis from a branch. Scratch that

*

A pair of hands dangling in the air trees make percussive: *across rough waters a music—*

The Breaking of an Enclosure
(for cicadas and hands)

FM radio—A distal mouth, static between leaves.

The hands are folded, enfolding silences, cicadas
tuned to 109.9.

Direction:

Say what you see in that hearing.

for Matt Marble

The Impossible Poem

"Can this be New Rochelle?" George asked J—. "I lived in a house on the water, near the harbor, in a small village." J— replied, "What village? What harbor?"
—Mary Oppen

This is true: the work before you is still the work ahead of me. It is not George Oppen (does it even need to be said) but something other than what that figure stands for. It is an alchemy of memory, both actual and "false." (I say "false" because it is not false—I have felt a stranger breathing down my neck, in a wind, a we, descending, as our gifts remain above us, ungrasped.)

It started simply. I wanted only to use "another's" words to cull memory—not to express it, but to excavate. It quickly became something else, or many things. Though I tried, I could never control it. Every move I made had multiple repercussions, often damaging, always damaging—it was Jack Spicer's chess game, the enemy pieces themselves laughing, threatening to end the game.

It started like this: Many years ago on the first day of Spring I was sitting haphazardly before two poems: Oppen's 'Disasters' and the first of Spicer's 'Two Poems for The Nation.' I wrote the line "In the notorious violence of birds" and crossed it out. I then wrote the line "Pieces of the past arising out of the rubble," and wrote many more lines after it until I lost my breath and my hands (not my own) were shaking. I called it a wolf assay. I called the poem 'My Own Private Idaho.'

The next day came, and then the day after, and then a week passed, then a month, and the next Spring became many Springs later. During this period, I continued to revise the poem, taking a line out here, replacing another there, drastically altering a section of stanzas and then rewriting them more or less as they were before, and so on, over and over. I would send out my newest revisions to friends—sometimes several a day—until all of them eventually stopped responding or commenting. I could never get it right—it still isn't. Here is one of the earliest versions of the opening stanza (I don't expect you, Oppen, to respond either):

> Pieces of the past rising from Joseph.
> Junked,
> an overturned Weremart cart

—Weremart, spelled as I have remembered it. I had come to associate this place—a supermarket in Caldwell where housewives shop—with wolves, the root of a savage becoming, so present in what lurks behind Idaho: *were*, Old English for "man," a cognate of Irish *fear* (Oppen: *wolf walks in my footprints fear fear*). But it was not until I started this essay that I realized Weremart was actually, and had always been, spelled W*a*remart.

Oppen: *Remember Yeats chained to a dying animal? . . . The animal's bare eyes in the woods—that's no joke.*

The poem continues:

> In Idaho wolf hides in mother
> and her hair unfolds beneath the metal
> of her helmet, and there's something about
>
> where a past and your pulse separate
> into two kinds of machine:
> the clunky and the jammed
>
> the ghosts and the guns that don't work
> when they don't have oil in the barrels
> and they don't have soldiers in the fields.

Apparently I had worried a lot over these stanzas. A few versions later they had been changed to:

in Idaho where there is
something about this separation
of the pulse with a past

as clunky and jammed as
a gun that don't work
when it don't have oil in its barrel

or a hunter's arm to cradle.
Dear killed hunter,
I made you up and

A variability of image: the heavy handed, politicized elements (helmet, oil barrel, soldiers) were just that: images. (Had I lost the finger with which one silently points to a soldier?) Yet in the second version these images' context was only replaced by another context, one which evokes my father (who had been a soldier in Vietnam, but who I remember as the hunter who shot himself in the cab of his truck many years before I started the poem).

This version continues its address to the hunter:

now I'm asking you a question
noone ever answered for me:
how come pop tastes so good?

In the field behind the school
you were vacated from my body.
In a secret cab of the Chevy.

In a cemetery where
present events defy us
and the past rests its corpses.

In a later version, the poem continues:

Oh floating wolfy,
your teats are metal and when
I was teething my gums

were so dry; now
all our ghosts can't evoke
an art that doesn't evoke

suspicion in this farmer's daughter
fingering the seems of
the future, the crow's

feet that stretch from the past.

My first gesture was to write toward primitive memory, toward "wolf" and "Idaho," using—with *usura*—the Oppen and Spicer I have inherited in the overpriced editions so widely available. It was to cling their disparate pieces together, to put them into a constellation. Yet the force of the bringing together—my force—was too much, too suffocating. Somehow, despite or because of myself, it has remained insistent, and continues to be—which is why, it seems, I cannot be finished with it.

Oppen: *I am sick with a poet's / vanity // legislators // of the unacknowledged.*

Yet I cannot *not* be aware of how inadequate my very *I* is in retelling the story of the poem's process—though I cannot seem to get around *I*. I have dismantled this essay, I have demolished this essay, I have put its shells back in new orders, yet it is never right—just as the poem was never right—I circle around the constellation of a presence, the broken constellation of a broken presence, but there is no final stroke to close the circle and *I* cannot close the circle.

Oppen: *What I couldn't write I scratched out.*

So I start over. Scratch that

So *he* starts over, moving forward. It is Oppen's poem now:

In an ocean confusing all our ghosts
can't evoke an art that doesn't evoke

Suspicion in this, father, fingering the seams
of the future—The crow drags its telephone
lines from the unacknowledged, a world so dreary

to which we descend
who have become strangers in this wind

As the revision continued, does it not seem as if he were trying to revert the language of the poem back to its sources? Compare the lines above to 'Disasters:'

of the unacknowledged

world it is   dreary
to descend

and be a stranger how
shall we descend

who have become strangers in this wind

Perhaps this is the question: Is there an Idaho to be found below Oppen's language? He had led me in equal measures of belief and doubt to find this Idaho, to bring it forth and place it at the side of whatever George Oppens may exist—

But that's not quite right. Yes, there was faith, there was doubt, but we cannot now place this beside any Oppen or thing. Instead, does it not seem that he was attempting to condense "our" language—already "others'"—to a different state of otherness? Or, in other words, wasn't I merely trying to rewrite 'Disasters,' and in the process squeeze Oppen out of the poem—to further other the poem's already absent author?

Oppen: *One sees a man in his place, which excludes us, as travelers through it.*

But we cannot let our story end there, in that space of both confirmation and negation. Backtrack a bit, to an earlier version of the poem which continues with an address to 'Disasters' itself:

> So, Dreary, do we descend
> as strangers through this wind
>
> or through the radios in our sitting rooms—
> Is my own room, where we assay
> *we*, an ancestral disorder,
>
> the promised gift after all
> stories end in good and
> impossible dimensions—

Can these "impossible dimensions" be true? Or,

Can this be true: When I started the poem on the first day of Spring some years earlier, I was living next door to the hotel where the Falstaff scenes in Gus Van Sant's film were shot—a fact I hadn't realized at the time. When I first saw *My Own Private Idaho*, it made a deep impression. In the film, Mike Waters, the narcoleptic street hustler played by River Phoenix, searches for his estranged mother in an attempt to recover his past out of the vagaries of memory. His search takes him between Portland, various parts of Idaho, all the way to Italy, and back to the streets of Portland. Throughout the film, as Waters' narcolepsy overcomes him and he passes out, grainy Super 8 footage of rolling cloudscapes, a decrepit house falling from the sky, demolishing itself through its own weight, and images of a young mother with her infant on the porch of that very house, are spliced into each other as he sleeps. Seen only in narcoleptic fits of dream, after falling with a thud in moments of extreme duress—Oppen in the foxhole, blasted, dreaming of his mother, or the wolf that hides under her helmet—we see Idaho, this ungraspable, private scape, in whose arms we never wake. In this same manner, our search—from line to line, poem to poem—can never recover the impossible place, the impossible poem. The last stanza of 'My Own Private Idaho,' through all its years remaining unchanged, continues:

> To what this is ancestral
> is the past surrounding us in Idaho:
> a wolf formed from clay
> hands stuffing mouths full of fur.

To Oppen

whose name escaped its sign, a
stranded star that scars
night's body. Shining just as bright

as skylit eyes, you're peeling open

I in silence can only point toward
your pointing. Darting away
who will find my arm embedded in the trees

felled to make the bird alight?
Who will find the swift tiger we write
to loose and propel and be

propelled by haunches sprung as wolfen wings?
Who can see the single ashen bird
in the dust of Father's arms beating

Father, who will fear not your fearful sheen
and peel our fingers from our nails
and nails from our teeth.

See Rimbaud's 'Phrases:' *Que j'aie réalisé tous vos souvenirs,—que je sois celle qui sait vous garrotter,—je vous étoufferai.* [Should I have realized all your memories,—should I be the one who can bind you hand and foot,—I shall strangle you.]

To Oppen

Enough of the ground we see
Enough disheveled nests in threadbare trees
cloud gently torn—In the ground we see

Enough mouths choked on bark
Enough mouths stuffed with fur
The wolf we thought each other to be

too much memory we no longer call our own—
This art's to follow the hand that leads
the fangs—who planted?—it's to trail our own feet

past pastoral wastes, walking, we trudge
through marrow of leaves, bending bone
Building a new image of our old house

stranded between *remembered* and *returning*
we'll say we've willed a new word for ourselves—
call it our name but never our home.

we'll call it the name for "We Are Not Home."

Key

16	3	2	13
5	10	11	8
9	6	7	12
4	15	14	1

you	Spicer	music	hands
wolf	sky	Idaho	fire
tree	Oppen	I	eye
stone	ocean	house	birds

birds—Call them mazes. One devours just as one enunciates.

Was it a tiger or my invention?
—Philip Jenks

eye—Simultaneously things. See **I**.

fire—A squaring of circles.

And there's no magic in our field, no
painting of the pasture or
fire. The blank picture is a sky
—Robert Duncan, 'The Fire'

hands—Often in pairs, often falling from branches like pears.

radio: "15 days of Christmas kill"
a simple past of finger's traces
emphatic thumbs, no faces
—ibid.

house—A house more elusive (allusive) than birds, is also opposed to the feet.

Thou think upon thies thre,
Wo we are,
Wo we ware,
Wo we shall be.
—Anonymous

I—See **I**.

Idaho—"Moments of a childhood are created as Edens, the mythic seed of a power in the story to come—"

> *The gravel path*
> *up a tiny hill huge*
> *to a house of 7*
> *a house of 5*
> *to crowd w/in a room*
> *a room of 5 then 4*
> *to the little creek that was a canal*
> —Anon.

music—One is never permitted to exit this Ark.

> *Hell is this:*
> *The lack of anything but the eternal to look at*
> *The expansiveness of salt*
> *The lack of any bed but one's*
> *Music to sleep in*
> —Spicer, 'Orfeo'

ocean—A nonsense syllable invented by the poet, meant to invoke or shatter. The arms must be used as propellants when reading.

> *across rough waters illumined*
> —Oppen

Oppen—An alter ego that can only fail as alter ego. These two syllables harden at the lips when spoken.

sky—That which is without need; self-sufficient.

The blank picture is the sky
—Anon.

Spicer—A cabinet, as well as the curios it contains. A radio that eats its own signal. The broken joints of Orpheus's fingers. One could invent any number of metaphors, and they would all be wrong.

stone—A nonsense syllable invented by the poet, meant to invoke or shatter. The arms must be used as propellants when reading.

if I stumble on a rock I speak / of rock
—Oppen

tree—Irrevocable clouds.

and thus the impression
of standing under a sky you can see
—Cole Swensen

wolf—A dying animal. Avail. Wolves are everywhere present, yet never quite seen.

you—See **thorn**.

Who is the third that walks always beside you?
When I count there are only you and I together
—T.S. Eliot

Addenda

To L.E.B.

Were the trains we heard approaching, never arriving,
The train we trail after, never catching
The sound we thought we heard, Father, the sound of
Your voice trailing off in present moments
Of nearly being present with you, not running after
But sitting still and waiting for you to pass through
A crowd of folded hands unfurling, palms flat
Mirrors refracting a face almost familiar among
So many familiar faces, lips open and closing
Soundlessly among you, Father, you open your throat

From a Screenplay Called 'The Empty Projector'

(the scene begins in darkness, tangled limbs: out of breath)

Spicer: Well, the bird's gone—the projector's off.

Oppen: (heavy breathing, consternation)

Spicer: Do you have anything left to say to me?

Oppen: (panting slows to silence)

Spicer: Well?

Oppen: Was the projector ever even on?

Spicer: There probably wasn't even a projector. (long silence) And there probably wasn't even a bird . . .

Oppen: It's just us . . .

Spicer: Alone together . . .

Oppen: Under the coil of these branches . . .

Spicer: What?

Oppen: Never mind.

(during the previous dialogue the outline of a tree emerges: make the image of the tree the absence of the tree's image—the absence of the absent tree being of course the house that houses the bird)

Spicer: (long silence) I guess I could share one of my poems with you.

Oppen: Sure.

Spicer: I didn't write it, actually.

Oppen: What's it called?

Spicer: '7-7-84.' Does this sound familiar?

Oppen: Of course—the day I died. (silence) What's this about?

Spicer: Well, let me explain some things first. In the poem I use the word "oricle," O-R-*I*-C-L-E, which is a homophone of "oracle," O-R-*A*-C-L-E, as well as "auricle," the external part of the ear. The prefix *ori*—as in *orificium vaginae*—refers to the mouth. (silence) So you can see the importance of the "oricle"—the site of magic and the orifice that gives, and receives.

Oppen: And consumes.

Spicer: Right. It consumes every bird—it vomits as it eats.

(here the film breaks, burnt by the projector's light)

(25 years elapse—we return to Spicer, who has just finished his recitation)

Oppen: (long silence) Who wrote that poem?

Spicer: (out of breath) I did.

Oppen: No you didn't. But there were some birds in it.

Spicer: No there wasn't!

Oppen: What, did you think that poem would please me?

Spicer: Father, I have no need to please ghosts.

Oppen: What are you talking about? That's all you professed to do while alive—

Spicer: But that's the difference. Before I died, right after I passed out in the elevator of my building—and the thing did rise and fall, you know, for hours—I was covered in shit and vomit and still clutching my radio and a chicken sandwich—rising and falling, ascending and descending . . . (long silence) What was I just talking about?

Oppen: Something about ghosts.

(cut to ghosts: I cannot see their faces—am I blinded?)

(another lapse—Oppen and Spicer reappear faceless)

Spicer: What was I just talking about?

Oppen: Something about birds.

Spicer: Right. That's the difference between the living and—

Oppen: But you aren't living.

Spicer: Of course—

Oppen: You were.

Spicer: I was not—haven't you ever read me?

Oppen: Never got around to it. But you were among the living and still are, contrary to what you think you mean.

Spicer: I don't get you. How can you paint me in such a tableau?

Oppen: Because I know what you are: a "you" that negates its you-ness. Just as in the masses of the living there is constant negation and denial of the second person in the shear weight of bodies corded to bodies . . .

Spicer: What?

Oppen: You are this absent "you" because you have lived among this massive gravity between any "us"—

Joseph: You're right.

Oppen: Ah! I see you never left!

Joseph: Nope.

Spicer: Fuck this.

(cut: an absence of image: the bright light of the empty projector)

The Impossible Poem

While I clearly remember writing the first draft of 'Our Own Private Idaho,' I cannot remember any particular instance of revising it, even though I have hundreds of variously typed, handwritten, struck-through, scratched out pages, as well as numerous electronic files that contain different versions. While searching through these remnants I found another poem, one I don't remember writing, with the title 'First of Wolf Assay:'

> Never achieving music. George Oppen
> leaving his desk for a death bed
> writes, "music that marvel."
> Thank you Stephen Cope, and thank you
> Mary.
>   My faux pas
> was a little garden.

This poem is dated almost two months before I started 'Wolf Assay.' 'Twenty-Six Fragments,' Oppen's last writings, faithfully transcribed by Mary Oppen and later edited by Stephen Cope, had recently been published. (Fragment #1: *Music, that marvel / trying to exist / out of this forest to come forth.*) 'First of Wolf Assay' continues:

>   Jack Spicer
> leans into my ear. He whispers,
> "scorpion tongues flower." His tongue seeps
> past my oricle, wetting my bed.
> It is made of sound. He licks it
> and every one of his fingers
> entering every orifice.
>   My
> faux pas was a lovely little garden

Thus the "oricle"—the mouth that both speaks and hears, consumed by Spicer "entering every orifice." But what is the "little garden"? Is it a tamed, tended plot set against Oppen's wild forest of music's origin? Is this the "faux pas" of the garden: its very littleness and loveliness? Is then the lovely little garden what we leave behind after Spicer's sexualized consumption of our mouth and ear—the instruments of our music? If so, would it seem that this poem articulates a scene of initiation at the gate of the forest—with Spicer and Oppen standing guard—and that the forest itself is the site of music in music's impossibility? Who then will be permitted to pass the gate and enter the forest, answering—

I am hesitating. How can I go on with this:

Who then will be permitted to pass the gate and call out in answer—

Answering what? And with whose lips—since ours, long chapped, have fallen, destroyed, devoured by Spicer, now silent—the consumer's silence now our very own—

It's all wrong—can we read "Oppen" for "Spicer"?

No—it's all wrong.

No.

It's—this is—is all wrong.

On Oppen's Bird

Wolves fell to the earth, created the earth to watch what would grow to the clouds, but they had no control over what sprung out of the ground: rotten beanstalks, a child's grotesque ear tilted skyward, etc. This is the first version of the myth of the world's origin. In the second version the wolves were already there, waiting when the earth was born, though what they were waiting for was uncertain. Actually, uncertainty and the inability to grasp the soundless snap of one moment bleeding into the next—forward motion, as of the walking body's fluidity—was the wolves' obsession. In a third version the wolves were not wolves at all, but birds. Or rather, the wolves were to birds as caterpillars are to moths. We, who always listen for the wolves, were born in that cocoon.

We could continue listing more versions, but these are enough. Oppen expressed this myth somewhat differently with the statement: *When the man writing is frightened by a word, he may have started.* The word is of course *wolf.* The word is of course *bird.* See the last lines of 'World, World,' a poem addressed to the birds of poetry:

> you, a body all verb
> walks in my footprints.
>
> My footprints, they you.

See Oppen's 'A Political Poem:' *wolf walks in my footprints fear fear*. It's my sense that Oppen's wolf, haunting the poet, was in turn haunted by a bird (a triangular knot that becomes a tangle when we add the second person, you). We know where the wolf is—behind some skin, hiding, silently observing—but what agent binds it to the bird? Is it what binds fire to smoke? Or is it what doesn't bind a fire hydrant to the thumbless man whose wrists are burning?

In the twelfth chapter of *Vita Nuova,* Dante presents the first poem in the book intended for Beatrice directly. Addressing the ballad itself, Dante instructs it to in turn address his beloved. The poem is thus the interface between the poet's you and I, and simultaneously the ballad's you is the you of the intended reader (Beatrice), and the you of the actual reader (us):

> first make a friend of love;
> perhaps to go alone would not be wise.

You is more than you, and I is what's between the I and the you as well as you: the immanent confusion of Love Itself. It is startling (from Middle English *stertlen*, "to run about," in turn from Old English *steartlien*, "to kick")—to confront you, to confront oneself, to make a friend of love. To be startled, to thrash ourselves out of our bodies, into each other, birds: Is this what frightens we poets—or "Love's faithful" as Dante has it—that violent avian molting we so desire, so need to, paradoxically, become what we are? In the following passage from 'George Oppen Has a Cold,' Gay Talese famously highlights Oppen's moving of *bird* through continual insertion, in a continual becoming:

> . . . and some will laugh about Oppen having gotten the word "bird" in the book—this being a favorite Oppen word. He often inquires of his poems, "How's your bird?"; and when he nearly drowned, he later wrote, "Just got a little water in my Bird"; and under a large photograph of him holding a Kalashnikov rifle, a photo that hangs in the home of a poet friend named J—, the inscription reads: "Shoot, J—! It's good for your bird." In the poem, 'Birthplace: New Rochelle,' Oppen sometimes alters the lyrics: *just say the word / and we'll take our Bird / down to Bodega Bay . . .*

Here conflated with New Rochelle, the site of the poet's origin, Bodega Bay is of course the township where Alfred Hitchcock set *The Birds*. In the film, several common species of shorebird attack the Bay's inhabitants, murdering hundreds, and imprisoning many more in their homes. The birds' attacks are sudden, inexplicable, and total. And, if I am remembering the film correctly, the birds arrive from the direction of the sea; this is significant, in light of Oppen's mention of Bodega Bay, because he himself called his boat—a boat being "a small vessel used for propelling on water"—Bird. Was Oppen, through naming, consciously harnessing the violent energy arriving from the sea, and, through Bird, projecting it back into itself? Or is this memory's distortion? Rachel Blau DuPlessis, aboard Bird, writes:

> George is on the sea, steering, the sea pulling: the poem changes force and weight at every word but moves continuing forward.

DuPlessis's statement can be rephrased in a string of three syllogisms—a syllogism being "a system of rules that a particular community recognizes as regulating the actions of its members and may enforce by the imposition of penalties:" 1) Sea, therefore Bird; 2) Bird, therefore flood; 3) Flood, therefore Oppen's 'Twenty-Six Fragments,' #11:

> *Our little bird: I*
> *feel all my*
> *boyhood in*
> *him*

(For "bird" read "wolf.")

A Letter to I.S. Belissop from George Oppen

Preface

When Rit Premnath and Avi Alpert, editors at *Shifter Magazine*, contacted me about contributing work to *Shifter* 13: *I.S. Belissop*, I had been working for well over two years on *In the Common Dream of George Oppen*. Since my project is cousins of a sort with work on I.S. Belissop, I was enthusiastic to participate, and to research any possible meetings or overlap Oppen may have had with Belissop. A connection between these two complex figures was confirmed almost immediately; what I found was the rather puzzling letter that follows. While the letter would seem to indicate that Oppen and Belissop may have had a deeper correspondence, there are no letters from Belissop among Oppen's surviving papers. To add to the mystery, the missive that follows is the only letter of Oppen's explicitly addressed to Belissop. It is quite clearly a draft, and there is no record of it having been revised and sent by Oppen, or received by Belissop.

About I.S. Bellisop, Alpert and Premnath have written: "While stranded in Dublin, Ohio on September 13th 2001 due to the grounding of all domestic flights in the US, the editors visited the local library. Thumbing through the card catalog, they found a reference to 'Other Possibilities,' by Indira Sylvia (I.S.) Bellisop, assigned the Dewey Decimal call number 125.20. Let alone the book, even this curious number inserted between 'Teleology' (124) and 'The Self' (126) has since been impossible to find in major libraries around the world. The book itself did not appear on the shelf, and the card, in classic Courier font, stated simply, 'Collected writings of Mozambique-born philosopher.'" (See *Shifter* 13 for a biographical sketch of Belissop.)

[Undated]

Sylvia:

Bellicose, possible, burst. I call you by your middle name from my own name—George Sylvia Oppen—to wrest us out of this forest to come forth into

~~the letters or limbs embrace, smother you, Indyra, I cannot not recall my failure, my guilt at having fallen open upon you white our voices heat crying Mary I thought you were her back pressed against my belly~~

the possible burst: will it be hair long and dark or silver, or my fingers running thru water, down along your shoulders will I follow, will I recall any of ~~your face~~ these parted full or chapped lips—Sylvia, you have no face and this is why your memory is a wolf~~—Mother, I'm seeing even you~~ beneath my thrusting abdomen ~~where is my penis? does it begin in the tree?~~

^*I'm thrusting, thrusting into what I came out of, and I cannot enter, no matter how deep I push I will not stay, I am coming and always coming, always about to arrive—but where is my penis? Is it buried in the tree? Are its branches extending over us, naked, birds' nests dropping like leaves? Should we call this Winter or Spring?*^

[unsigned]

A Chronology

circa 41,000 BCE—A woman holds a mollusk's shell up to her ear, marking the beginning of the ocean. Rilke reconfigures this moment in the opening of *Sonnets to Orpheus*: "O hoher Baum im Ohr!" [A tree arises in the ear].

375 BCE—Startled at its own image, a centaur darts out of the cave and stumbles to its death over the cliff's edge. The delayed thud, echoing through the canyon, is Plato's laughter.

1170 CE—Metaphor makes its first literary appearance, through the string the two lovers tie between each other (via *le rossignol*), in Marie de France's 'Laüstic.'

1797—Samuel Taylor Coleridge, passed out in a narcotic stupor after jotting the fragment 'Kubla Khan,' has the following dream:

> *Trudging up a long hill. As I climb, the path is murkier, stickier, slowing my step. Soon I'm wading through what I understand to be shark marrow, which boils me, starching my pants. They cling tight below my knees. I struggle to cast them off. Finally I do. Naked then, I ascend further, until coming to a kind of shed, its floor caked shin-deep with bone, crushed to powder. In the center of the dank room is a glass encasement of a large but broken animal skeleton, in the shape of a shipwrecked hull, labeled "Shark Exoskeleton." I circle the case, the powder cooling my feet.*

circa 1950s—Robin Blaser reinvents Idaho. Of his birthplace he writes: *the absence preceded the place.*

1963—Gilbert Sorrentino publishes favorable reviews of both *The Materials* and *HEADS OF THE TOWN UP TO THE ÆTHER* in *Kulchur* #9. In his response to Sorrentino, George Oppen writes, "I've never read Spicer, but will."

1965—Jack Spicer fatally collapses in the elevator of a San Francisco apartment building. As if haywire, the elevator rises and falls for several hours. His unconscious, barely living body—covered in its own shit and vomit—rises and falls. When the medics finally arrive, he is found clutching a radio and a chicken sandwich.

1984—Oppen dies of dementia, unaware of where or who he is. His last lines are:

Never achieving music
George Oppen died in Idaho, he
Writes 'music that marvel'
—7/8/84

early 2000s—Startled, I wake: I'm in the old Weremart in Caldwell again, alone, sorting through the notebooks in the stationary aisle, when I begin to notice they're all filled with the markings of a familiar hand.

CPSIA information can be obtained
at www.ICGtesting.com
Printed in the USA
LVOW08s1550070217
523493LV00001B/181/P